A Guide for Using

The Magic School Bus® Lost in the Solar System

in the Classroom

Based on the book written by Joanna Cole

This guide written by **Ruth M. Young, M.S. Ed.**

Teacher Created Materials, Inc.
6421 Industry Way
Westminster, CA 92683
www.teachercreated.com
©1996 Teacher Created Materials, Inc.
Reprinted, 2002, a
Made in U.S.A.
ISBN-1-57690-086-X

Illustrated by
Sue Fullam

Edited by
Walter Kelly, M.A.

Cover Art by
Dianne Birnbaum

Table of Contents

Introduction 3

Planet Data 4

Before the Book (Pre-reading Activities) 5

   ✦ Making scale models of the planets and solar system . . . .

About Author Joanna Cole 9

Book Summary 10

Hands-On Lessons:

   ✦ Planets on the Move 11

      (drawing orbits of the planets)

   ✦ Spinning Earth 13

      (investigating Earth's motion)

   ✦ 3-2-1 Blast Off! 15

      (building and testing a rocket)

   ✦ Keeping a Space Log 19

      (recording the trip through space)

   ✦ You Are Go for Launch! 22

      (presenting a play about a trip to the moon)

   ✦ Touring the Inner Orbits 30

      (learning about the sun, Mercury, Venus, and Mars)

   ✦ Visiting the Giants 33

      (comparing Jupiter, Saturn, Uranus, and Neptune)

   ✦ The Dark Planet 36

      (learning about Pluto)

After the Book (Post-reading Activity)

   ✦ Comets 39

      (making a comet and orbits)

Unit Assessment (Culminating Activity)

   ✦ Vacation in Space 41

Resources

   ✦ Related Books and Materials 43

      (annotated list of related books, periodicals, and materials)

Answer Key 45

Introduction

The use of literature can enhance the study of science. The key to selecting these books is to check them for scientific accuracy and appropriateness for the level of the students. *The Magic School Bus*® series, written by Joanna Cole, is an outstanding example of books which can help students enjoy and learn about science. These books are delightfully written and scientifically accurate, thanks to the thorough research done by the author as she writes each of her books.

This Science/Literature Unit is directly related to *The Magic School Bus*® *Lost in the Solar System*. It is designed to help you present exciting lessons for your students so that they can develop their understanding and appreciation of the solar system. The activities in this unit are particularly appropriate for intermediate and middle grades.

Internet Extenders

Today, many classrooms are connected to the Internet, which puts students in touch with worldwide resources. As with selecting the literature, the author of this unit has searched the Internet to find quality Web sites that directly relate to the topics covered in this book. This supplemental information helps to expand the students' knowledge of the topic, as well as make them aware of the many valuable resources to be found on the Internet. Some Web sites lend themselves to group research; others are best viewed by the entire class. If available, use a large-screen monitor when the entire class is viewing a Web site and discussing its content.

Internet Extenders are included throughout the unit. These are special sections which note outstanding Web sites and include suggestions for incorporating Web site information into the lessons. Where appropriate, a Technology Extender, such as the use of video cameras, may also be suggested in the lessons.

Although these Web sites have been carefully selected, they may not exist forever. One method of assuring that Web site information will continue to be available for a class is to use a program (if available) or browser which enables one to download and save a single Web page or entire site. Teacher Created Materials attempts to offset the ongoing problem of sites which move, "go dark," or otherwise leave the Internet after a book has been printed. If you attempt to contact a Web site listed in this unit and find that it no longer exists, check the TCM home page at www.teachercreated.com for updated URL's for this book.

Planet Data

To the Teacher: *This chart should be distributed to the students when they begin their Space Log (page 20). They can use it as a reference when adding descriptions of each planet they visit during this unit. Discuss the chart with the students after distributing it so they will understand how to interpret the data.*

Categories	Mercury	Venus	Earth	Mars	Jupiter	Saturn	Uranus	Neptune	Pluto
Diameter in Miles: (kilometers)	3,050 (4,880)	7,563 (12,100)	7,973 (12.756)	4,246 (6,794)	89,365 (142,984)	75,335 (120,536)	31,938 (51,100)	30,938 (49,500)	1,438 (2,300)
Diameters relative to Earth's	.38	.95	1.0	.53	11.2	9.4	4	3.9	.18
Average Distance from sun in millions of miles: (Kilometers)	36 (57.9)	67 (108.2)	93 (149.6)	142 (227.9)	486 (778.3)	893 (1,429)	1,797 (2,875)	2,815 (4,504)	3,688 (5,900)
Relative to Earth's	0.4 AU*	0.7 AU	1.0 AU	1.5 AU	5.2 AU	9.6 AU	19.3 AU	30.3 AU	39.7 AU
Length of year (trip around sun)	88 days	224.7 days	365.3 days	687 days	11.86 years	29.46 years	84 years	165 years	248 years
Length of Day (turn around once on axis)	59 days	243 days Retro **	23h 56m	24h 37m	9h 55m	10h 40m	17h 18m Retro**	16h 7m	6 days 9h 18m Retro**
Gravity at Surface	.38 g	.91 g	1.00 g	.38 g	2.53 g	1.07 g	.91 g	1.16 g	.05 g (?)
Number of Moons	0	0	1	2	16	18	15	8	1
Number of Rings	0	0	0	0	3	1,000 (?)	11	4	0

*AU = Astronomical Unit, average distance between Earth and sun which is 93 million miles (149.6 million kilometers). The data below each planet shows its distance in astronomical units.
**Retro means "retrograde" or backward motion from the rest of the planets. Earth turns (rotates) on its axis from west to east; planets which have retrograde motion rotate east to west.

Statistics for the planets were taken from the most recent information available from NASA and other reliable sources. You may find different data in recent articles since this information is continuously being revised through the use of new equipment, such as the Hubble Telescope. Photographs of the planets are available from JPL and CORE (see Resource section). These photographs will enhance this unit by enabling the students to view the planets as they study them.

The Solar System

Before you begin reading *The Magic School Bus® Lost in the Solar System,* you need to know the size of the planets and their distances from the sun and each other. Complete the activities "How Big Are the Planets?" and "Planets' Distances from the Sun." (pages 5 and 8)

How Big Are the Planets?

Before making a scale model of the planets, show how big you think they are. The size of the Earth has been drawn to give you a scale for the planets. Draw the remaining planets (**Mercury, Venus, Mars, Jupiter, Saturn, Uranus, Neptune,** and **Pluto**) to show how large they are compared to Earth. Be sure to label each planet.

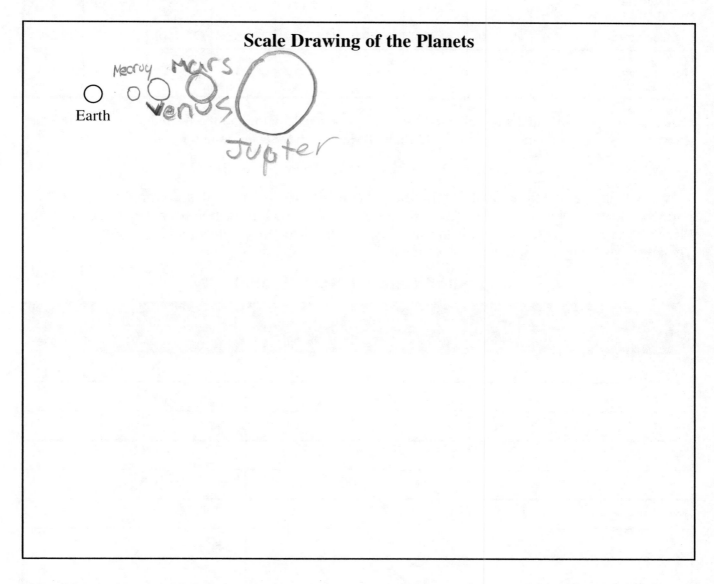

Now, use the information on the next page to help you make paper scale models of the planets. When you are finished with that project, compare the drawing you have just made with your model planets to see how accurate you were.

Making a Scale Model of the Planets

To the Teacher: Have all the students complete the chart to calculate the scale model size of all the planets. Divide the students into nine groups and assign each group a planet to construct. Decide what colors of paper will be used for each planet. Blue would be most appropriate for Earth and black for Pluto. The four largest planets will need to be drawn on butcher paper. Jupiter and Saturn will be semicircles, and Neptune and Uranus will be large circles.

Diameters of the Planets

Planet	Mercury	Venus	Earth	Mars	Jupiter	Saturn	Uranus	Neptune	Pluto
Diameter in Miles:	3,050	7,563	7,973	4,246	89,365	75,335	31,938	30,938	1,438
(Kilometers)	(4,880)	(12,100)	(12,756)	(6,794)	(142,984)	(120,536)	(51,100)	(49,500)	(2,300)
Diameter relative to Earth's	.38		1.0						

Calculate each planet's diameter relative to Earth's. Use a calculator and the formula below to find the answers; then record them on the chart. Earth and Mercury have been done for you.

Planet's Diameter ÷ Earth's Diameter = Diameter relative to Earth's.

Now, calculate the size for each planet for your scale model, using Earth's diameter to set the scale. Earth's diameter will be reduced to 10 cm for this scale. Use the information from the Diameters of the Planets chart to complete the chart below and calculate the size of the radius for each planet model. The Earth has been done for you as an example.

Planet Data for Scale Model

	List Planets Largest to Smallest	Diameter Relative to Earth's	x 5 cm = Radius for Circle
1			
2			
3			
4			
5	Earth	1.00	5 cm
6			
7			
8			
9			

(See Answer Key for more information.)

Making a Scale Model of the Planets *(cont.)*

Materials: colored paper for each planet, including butcher paper for 4 largest planets, 4 meter sticks, 15 yd. (13.5 m) of string, 4 index cards, hole punch, five pencil compasses, Diameters of the Planets (page 6), scissors, tape

Procedure: Use the pencil compass to draw the smaller planets on the colored paper. The four largest planets will need to be drawn according to the following directions.

✧ Cut pieces of string the length of the radius of the largest planets plus about 4 in. (10 cm).

✧ Write the names of the planets and the lengths of the radius (for this scale model) on the index cards. Punch a hole in the middle of one long edge of the card and tie a string to it.

✧ Tie a loop in the end of the string so a pencil can be placed in it. When the string is stretched to its full length it should equal the radius needed for this model.

✧ Pin the colored paper to a bulletin board or place it on the floor. Center the index card at the top of the long edge or center of the paper and hold it so it will not move. Place the pencil in the loop and stretch the string. Draw a semicircle for Jupiter and Saturn.

✧ When drawing Neptune or Uranus, place the card in the center of the paper and tack or hold it in place. Stretch the string with the pencil and draw a large circle.

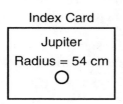

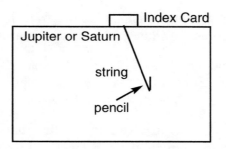

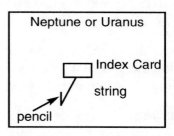

Cut out the planet and then label it with its name and diameter in miles and kilometers. Tape the planets together so they can be compared, superimposing them as shown in the drawing below.

Guess how many Earths fit across the diameter of Jupiter *before* measuring. _____

Use the Earth model to measure how many will fit across Jupiter._____

(1) **Earth**
(2) **Venus**
(3) **Mars**
(4) **Mercury**
(5) **Pluto**

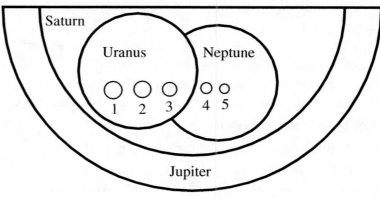

Making a Scale Model of the Solar System

To the Teacher: *Have all students complete the data on the chart below. Divide the students into nine groups and assign each group a different planet for which they are to construct a scale model of its distance from the sun.*

Planets' Distances from the Sun

Distance from sun	Mercury	Venus	Earth	Mars	Jupiter	Saturn	Uranus	Neptune	Pluto
millions of miles (Kilometers)	36 (57.9)	67 (108.2)	93 (149.6)	142 (227.9)	486 (778.3)	893 (1,429)	1,797 (2,875)	2,815 (4,504)	3,688 (5,900)
Relative to Earth's	0.4 AU		1.0 AU						

Astronomers use the Earth's distance from the sun as a standard for all the other planets. They call this distance one Astronomical Unit (AU). Use a calculator and the formula below to complete the astronomical units for the planets on the chart. Mercury and Earth are already done for you.

Planet's Distance ÷ Earth's Distance = _____ AU

Materials: 300 ft. (100 m) string, nine meter sticks, nine pieces of heavy cardboard 5 in. x 8 in. (12.5 cm x 20 cm), nine metal washers, copies of Planets' Distances from the Sun chart

Procedure: Label each cardboard with a planet's name and distance from the sun in miles and kilometers. Cut a piece of string the length of the AU for each planet and attach it to the cardboard. Wind the string around the cardboard and attach the metal washer to its end to keep it from fraying.

Closure: Go outside to stretch out the strings. Even though the planets do not travel in a line in space, place them in a line for this activity to compare their distances from each other. Select two people to stand side by side to represent the sun. Let one "sun" hold the ends of the strings of the four inner planets as each is unwound, beginning with Mercury. Now, add the string for Jupiter, letting the second "sun" hold the end of that string. Compare how close the four inner planets are compared to the distance between Mars and Jupiter. This space is not empty but is the location of the Asteroid Belt.

Now, add the remaining planets. Notice how far Pluto is from the sun. The sun would appear as a faint star from Pluto. On this scale, the nearest star to our solar system would be 174 miles (2,784 km)!

Internet Extender

Activity Summary: After laying out the solar system to this scale, share the information found at the following Web site which uses a scale of 1 step = 1 million miles. The time it would take to travel to planets beyond Venus by car or jet at this scale is given.

How Big Is Our Solar System?

http://www.dustbunny.com/afk/planets/howbig.htm

Take a trip through the solar system using a scale where each step = 1 million miles.

About Author Joanna Cole

Joanna Cole was born on August 11, 1944, in New York. She attended the University of Massachusetts and Indiana University before receiving her B.A. from the City College of University of New York in 1967.

Joanna Cole loved science as a child. "I always enjoyed explaining things and writing reports for school. I had a teacher who was a little like Ms. Frizzle. She loved her subject. Every week she had a child do an experiment in front of the room and I wanted to be that child every week," she recalls. It's no surprise that when she was a child Cole's favorite book was *Bugs, Insects, and Such.*

Ms. Cole has worked as an elementary school teacher, a librarian, and a children's book editor. Combining her knowledge of children's literature with her love of science, she decided to write children's books. Her first book was *Cockroaches* (1971), which she wrote because there had never been a book written about the insect before. "I had ample time to study the creature in my low-budget New York apartment!"

Teachers and children have praised Ms. Cole's ability to make science interesting and understandable. Her *Magic School Bus®* series has now made science funny as well. Cole says that before she wrote this series, she had a goal to write good science books telling stories that would be so much fun to read that readers would read them even without the science component.

Readers across the country love the *Magic School Bus®* series and enjoy following the adventures of the wacky science teacher, Ms. Frizzle. Joanna Cole works closely with Bruce Degen, the illustrator for this series, to create fascinating and scientifically accurate books for children.

At times, even a successful writer finds it scary to begin writing a new book. That was the way Ms. Cole felt before beginning to write the *Magic School Bus®* series. She says, "I couldn't work at all. I cleaned out closets, answered letters, and went shopping—anything but sit down and write. But eventually I did it, even though I was scared."

Joanna Cole says kids often write their own *Magic School Bus®* adventures. She suggests they just pick a topic and a place for a field trip. Do a lot of research about the topic. Think of a story line and make it funny. Some kids even like to put their own teachers into their stories.

The Magic School Bus® Lost in the Solar System

by Joanna Cole
(Scholastic, 1990)
(Canada, Scholastic; UK, Scholastic Ltd; AUS, Ashton Scholastic Party Ltd.)

The students in Ms. Frizzle's class are studying the solar system. What better way to learn about this topic than to go to the local planetarium? Of course, no field trip with "The Friz" ever goes as planned. When they find the planetarium is closed for repairs, the *Magic School Bus®* saves the day by turning into a rocket that blasts off into space. Teacher and students are now on the trip of a lifetime, viewing the planets of our solar system close up.

The first sign that they are in space is when the students discover they are floating, since they are beyond Earth's gravity. They view the beautiful Earth far below them, and Ms. Frizzle points out the oceans, clouds, and land.

No field trip would be complete without making a few stops along the way. The first one is on the moon, where the students are delighted to find they are much lighter than they were on Earth.

Back in the bus, they pass the sun and observe solar flares and sunspots. They avoid stopping on the sun and Mercury, which are much too hot. The bus dips below the clouds of Venus to see its dry, desert-like surface. Although it is the same size as the Earth, this planet is definitely not a place to get out and explore.

The next planet they visit is Mars, which has polar ice caps like Earth's and *two* moons. Mars also has a long canyon and erosion patterns which show it once had water on its surface. The bus lands so the students can see the red soil which has large amounts of iron in it which have rusted from the moisture in the atmosphere. The sky is pink because of the dust blown up in the air by strong winds.

Now, the rocket/bus leaves these inner planets behind and enters the asteroid belt. This is an area of thousands of chunks of material which never formed into a planet. Suddenly, one of the small asteroids hits the bus taillight and breaks it. Ms. Frizzle puts on a space suit and goes outside the bus to repair it. This is not a good idea, since another passing asteroid cuts her tether line and she floats away from the bus.

The students are now on their own, lost in the solar system! A visiting student, Janet, discovers Ms. Frizzle's lesson book and takes over teaching the students about the planets. They view the biggest planet, Jupiter, and are surprised to see the Great Red Spot, which is a swirling storm in its upper atmosphere. Next, they pass Saturn with its rings of rock, ice, and dust. Uranus and Neptune come into view, and like Jupiter and Saturn, are huge balls of gas. The smallest planet of the solar system, Pluto, is the last one they see before finding out how to use the autopilot. They punch in "Asteroid Belt," and the bus turns around and zooms back to the asteroid belt. There they rescue Ms. Frizzle, return safely back to school, and build a giant solar system mobile to show where they have been on their trip.

Drawing the Planets' Orbits

Ms. Frizzle is preparing her students for a field trip to the planetarium to see a sky show about the Solar System. She explains that an orbit is the path of a planet or other object around the sun. One of her students, John, wrote a report about the solar system and described it as the sun and all the bodies that orbit around it. These include nine planets, their moons, the asteroids, and comets.

Let's do an activity which shows what the planets' orbits look like from space.

Materials: butcher paper—36 in. x 80 in. (90 cm x 200 cm), Orbits of the Planets chart (page 12), pencil compass, T pin, string, pencil

Procedure: Pin the butcher paper to the bulletin board. Find the center of the paper and place a small x there to represent the sun. Follow the instructions on the next page. A drawing of what the finished project should look like is shown below. (This drawing is not to scale, and the orbits of Neptune and Pluto will be much farther from the sun than shown here.)

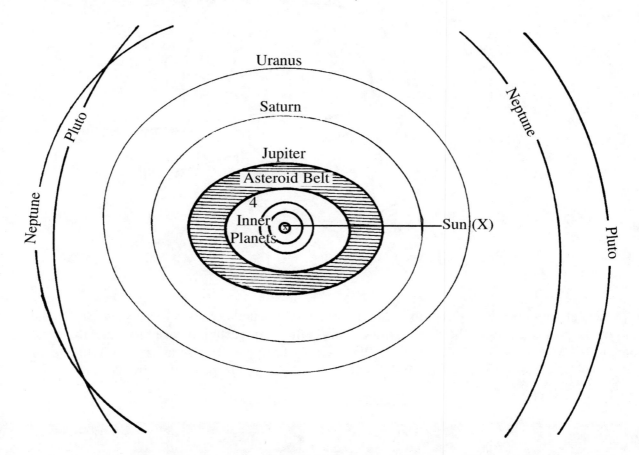

Closure: Look at the orbits and notice that those of Neptune and Pluto overlap. This brings Pluto closer to the sun during part of its journey around the sun. Pluto moved inside Neptune's orbit in 1979 and will not be outside it until 1999. The last time this happened was when George Washington was a boy. Will Pluto ever hit Neptune? No, Pluto's orbit tilts, missing Neptune's, and they are too far apart (remember the model of the solar system activity showing this distance).

Show where Ms. Frizzle and her students are by pinning a picture of their *Magic School Bus*® to their location on this orbit drawing and tracing their path as you travel with them.

Drawing the Planets' Orbits *(cont.)*

Instructions: Measure the location of the center of the orbits from the sun's position (X) by using the Orbit Offset data. The drawing below shows where this will be for the four inner planets using the scale of orbit radius from the chart. Notice that the offset positions for the first three planets are so little that the center for their orbits will be at the X (sun). Set the compass for Mercury's orbit for a radius of 9 mm, place the point of the compass on the X, and draw the circle. Repeat this for the orbits of Venus and Earth, using the lengths for their radius as shown on the chart.

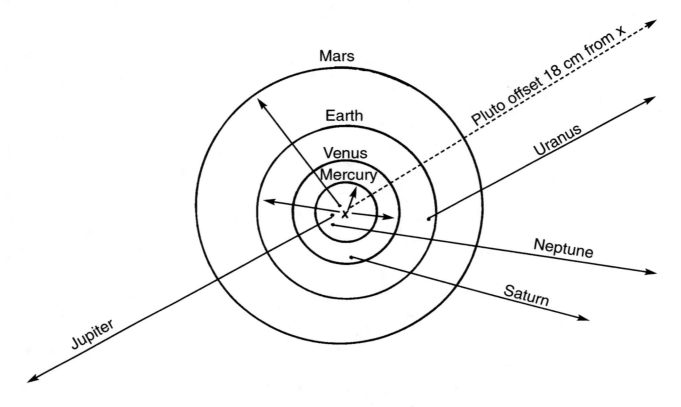

The planets after Mars have orbits too large to draw with a pencil compass. Use string, measured to the length of the radius, to make the larger orbits. This is the same technique used to make the large planets in the Making a Scale Model of the Planets activity (page 7). Use a T pin to hold one end of the string at the offset point and stretch the string with the pencil to make the circle or arc.

Orbits of the Planets

Distance from sun	Mercury	Venus	Earth	Mars	Jupiter	Saturn	Uranus	Neptune	Pluto
millions of miles (Kilometers)	36 (57.9)	67 (108.2)	93 (149.6)	142 (227.9)	486 (778.3)	893 (1,429)	1,797 (2,875)	2,815 (4,504)	3,688 (5,900)
Orbit Offset (in.) (mm)	.05 1 mm	.005 .1 mm	.016 .4 mm	.12 3 mm	.15 4 mm	.52 13 mm	.84 21 mm	.25 6 mm	7.1 180 mm
Orbit Radius (in.) (cm)	.36 (.9 cm)	.67 (1.7 cm)	.93 (2.4 cm)	1.42 (3.6 cm)	4.84 (12.3 cm)	8.87 (22.5 cm)	17.84 (45.4 cm)	27.96 (71 cm)	34.2 (87 cm)

Investigating Earth's Motions

Before going on their field trip to the planetarium, Ms. Frizzle and her students had studied how the Earth moves. Phoebe had written a report about what causes day and night on Earth. She said that the side of the Earth facing the sun has day, and when that side turns away from the sun, it is night.

Let's do an experiment to see how this works.

What Causes Day and Night?

Materials: globe, index card, bright light (such as an overhead projector)

Procedure: Draw a ¾ inch (2 cm) picture of a person on the index card and cut it out. Pretend this person is you and stick this picture to the globe where you live. Darken the room and shine the bright light on the globe. Slowly rotate the globe so that you are in the light (day) and then in the dark (night).

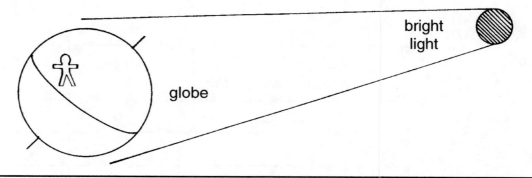

Which Way Do We Go?

Go outside in the early morning when the sun has risen; notice where it is located (low in the eastern sky). Look again later in the day and observe which way the sun has moved (west). Move your arm across the sky to show the path the sun took across the sky. Now, pretend you can speed up the Earth. Rotate your body so the sun will seem to be moving across the sky toward the west. Which way did you have to rotate? The sun appears to move east to west because we see it from Earth, which is rotating west to east.

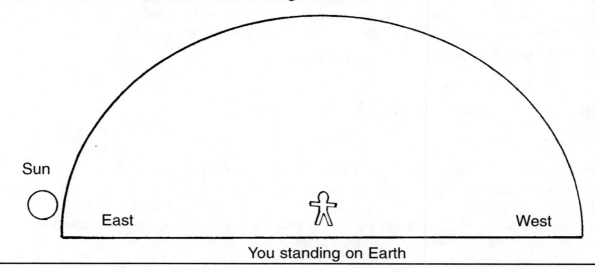

How Fast Are We Moving?

The Earth is shaped like a ball, and the equator is an imaginary circle between the North and South Poles. You need to find the *circumference* (distance around a circle) of the equator to calculate the speed of the Earth. Do the following activity to discover how to find the circumference by just knowing the diameter of a circle.

To the Teacher: *Students should measure the circles in metrics for better accuracy.*

Materials: tape measure, blank paper, pencil compass, calculator

Procedure: Use the compass to draw three circles with diameters of 5, 8, and 12 cm. Write the size of the diameters on the circles. Cut out the circles and tape them to a table to measure them. Stand the tape measure on its edge and wrap it carefully around the circle to find its circumference. Repeat this several times to be sure you are accurate and then record the circumference. Now, make a circle with a different diameter and measure its circumference.

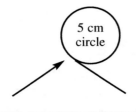

tape measure wrapped
around circle
(See Answer Key)

Circumference (measured to nearest mm.)	÷ Diameter	= Results
Circle 1 _____	5 cm	
Circle 2 _____	8 cm	
Circle 3 _____	12 cm	
Circle 4 _____ (your choice)	__ cm	

Use a calculator to discover the relationship between the diameter and the circumference. Divide the circumference by the diameter and record the results. Did you notice that the results are always about 3.14? Long ago mathematicians discovered that no matter what the size of the circle, the circumference was always 3.14 times as large as the diameter. This number is referred to by the Greek letter π (pi) and can be used to find the circumference of Earth.

Diameter of Earth _____ mi. (km) x 3.14 = _____ mi. (km) Circumference at Equator.

To find the speed of the Earth at the equator, complete the following:

Circumference _____ ÷ _____ Number of hours in a day = _____ mi. (km) per hour.

Closure: Since the circles of circumference get smaller toward the poles, there is less distance to travel, and thus the speed decreases. For example, at 45 degrees latitude, you would be traveling only half as fast as you do at the equator, and at the poles you would not be moving at all. To prove this to yourself, line up pieces of tape on the globe at the poles, equator, and 45 degrees north and south latitude. Spin the globe at a constant rate and watch the dots move. Which dot is going the fastest?

Building Rockets

When Ms. Frizzle drove the *Magic School Bus*® to the planetarium, she discovered that it was closed for repairs. Never one to pass up an opportunity for an exciting field trip, "The Friz" turned the Magic Bus into a rocket and blasted off into space.

Rocket Facts

The history of rockets began about two thousand years ago. One of the first devices to use the principles of rocketry was a wooden bird built by a Greek named Archytas in 400 B.C. He made a wooden pigeon suspended on wires and propelled by escaping steam.

About three hundred years later, another Greek, Hero, invented a similar rocketlike device which was a sphere mounted on top of a water kettle. When the water was heated to a boil, steam was fed into the sphere by pipes and escaped through L shaped tubes on opposite sides of the sphere. This allowed the gas to escape and provided the thrust needed to rotate the sphere.

Hero Engine

Rockets were used in warfare and fireworks by the Chinese as early as 1232. In 1898 a Russian schoolteacher, Konstantin Tsiolkovsky, proposed the idea of space exploration by rocket. He wrote a paper in 1903, suggesting the use of liquid propellants for rockets to send them out into space. He has been called the father of modern astronautics.

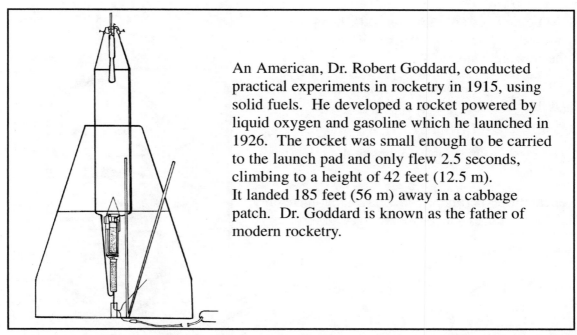

An American, Dr. Robert Goddard, conducted practical experiments in rocketry in 1915, using solid fuels. He developed a rocket powered by liquid oxygen and gasoline which he launched in 1926. The rocket was small enough to be carried to the launch pad and only flew 2.5 seconds, climbing to a height of 42 feet (12.5 m). It landed 185 feet (56 m) away in a cabbage patch. Dr. Goddard is known as the father of modern rocketry.

The science of rocketry was first recorded in 1687 in a book written by the great English scientist Sir Isaac Newton. His book described three principles which are now called Newton's Laws of Motion.

Newton's Laws of Motion

1. *An object at rest will stay at rest unless force moves it. An object moving in a straight line will continue in a straight line unless acted upon by a force.*

2. *The change of motion depends upon the amount of force and the mass of the object.*

3. *For every action there is always an opposite and equal reaction.*

Let's do two simple experiments to demonstrate Newton's three laws of motion.

Making a Hero Engine

Materials: small plastic water bottle, 1 ft. (30 cm) heavy string, small metal washer, nail or awl, hammer, masking tape

Procedure: Punch a hole in the center of the cap of the water bottle with the nail or awl and then feed the string through the hole. Tie the washer on the end of the string inside the cap. Poke holes in four spots, equally spaced, about ½ in. (1 cm) from the bottom of the bottle. Wrap masking tape around the bottom of the bottle to cover the holes, overlapping the end of the tape so it can be pulled off quickly.

Go outside and work with a partner to do the rest of this experiment. Fill the bottle with water, put the cap on it and hold it by the end of the string at arm's length from your body. Have your partner pull off the masking tape then let the bottle hang from the string. Watch to see what happens as the water flows from the bottle. Did you notice that it spun around fast at first, then slowed down as the water level dropped? Which way did the bottle rotate? Repeat the experiment several times to observe it more carefully.

Applying Newton's Laws

First law: The bottle does not move until the holes are uncovered and water flows out. It rotates because a force is exerted by the flowing water.

Second law: The speed or rotation slows as the fuel (water) decreases and thus becomes less able to push the mass (bottle and water).

Third law: The bottle rotates in the opposite direction from the streams of water.

Closure: Repeat this experiment with bottles that have only two holes in them. What changes did you see?

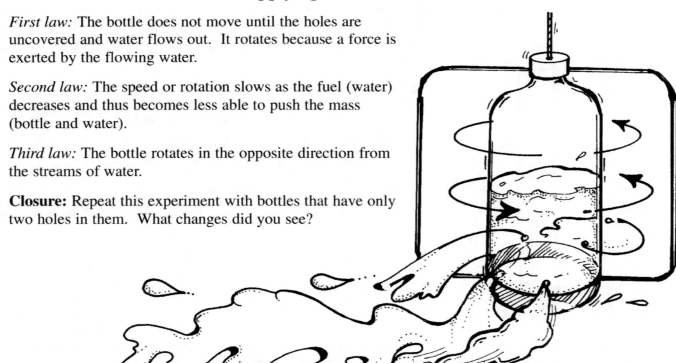

Making a Balloon Rocket

Rockets were sent to the moon between 1966 and 1972. The American *Apollo* missions made six landings on the moon, the first coming in July, 1969. Trips to the moon required rockets with several stages to provide enough thrust to get away from Earth's gravity and send the rocket to the moon.

See if you can experiment with an inflated balloon to make a rocket engine and then explain how this demonstrates Newton's three laws of motion.

Materials: one balloon, ½ drinking straw, 15 ft. (4.5 m) heavy string, scissors, clear tape

Procedure: Work with a partner to thread the string through the straw. Attach the string to the backs of two chairs and then separate the chairs to stretch the string as tight as possible. Inflate the balloon only part way. Hold the balloon closed while your partner tapes it to the straw. Be sure the straw is at the beginning of the string and the opening of the balloon faces away from the direction you want your rocket to go. Release the balloon to let the air escape. How far did the balloon go?

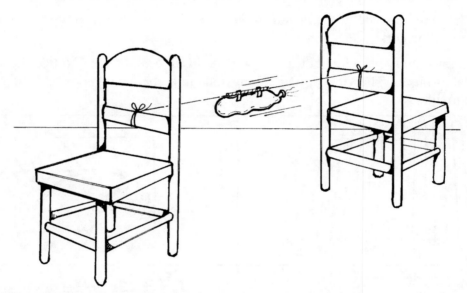

Remove the balloon and inflate it with more air this time to see if it goes the same distance. Mark where it stopped on the string.

Closure: On another paper, make a drawing of what happened in your experiment and describe which laws of motion were being demonstrated in each step. (See Answer Key)

Challenge: Try balloons of different sizes and shapes to see if you can perfect your rocket, just as real scientists do. Make a lightweight spaceship to fasten to your balloon rocket.

Internet Extender

Activity Summary: Scan down this list at this Web site to *Make a Pop Rocket!* This leads to simple instructions for building a rocket from paper, film canister, and effervescing (fizzing) antacid tablets. It also provides an explanation for how this works according to Newton's laws and shows a real example of the Delta rocket launching *Deep Space 1* satellite.

Build a Bubble Powered Rocket

http://kidsastronomy.miningco.com/kidsteens/ktschool.kidsastronomy/msub5.htm

---

Making Rocket Fuel

We have seen how Newton's third law of motion (for every action there is always an equal and opposite reaction) has worked in our previous two experiments. In space, however, there is no gravity to force water from a container, nor is there oxygen to fill a balloon.

Ordinary fuel for jets needs oxygen to burn. In space we need a rocket engine which carries its own oxygen supply. Many such engines rely on mixing two chemicals to produce oxygen which is then used to burn the fuel and create expanding gases that will propel the rocket.

Let us see if we can create a liquid fuel rocket engine that produces its own gas pressure to propel the rocket. (To avoid a mess inside, this experiment is best conducted outside.)

Materials: one 16.9 fl. oz. (500 mL) plastic water bottle, a cork to fit the bottle opening, a dozen round-barreled pencils, baking soda (sodium bicarbonate), vinegar, and a measuring cup

Procedure: 1. Line the pencils up parallel to one another and about one inch (2.5 cm) apart.

2. Using a paper cone as a funnel, pour $1/4$ cup of baking soda into the bottle.

3. Stand to one side of the pencils, pour about $1/4$ cup vinegar in the bottle and quickly place the cork in it.

4. Immediately place the bottle on the pencils and stand back. Notice the action which takes place. The vinegar and baking soda mix chemically, creating the gas carbon dioxide.

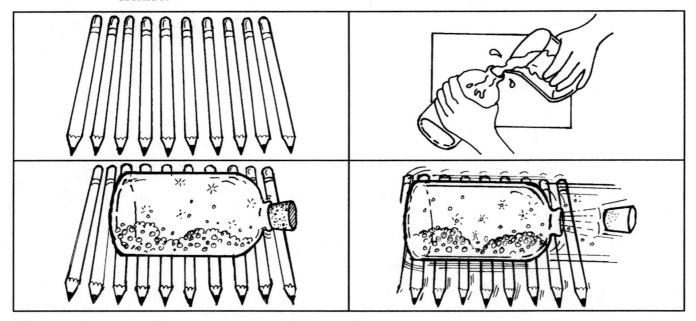

Closure: Tell what you saw happen and explain the reaction using Newton's Laws of Motion.

Internet Extender

Activity Summary: Learn about rockets of the future as you travel through this Web site. Pictures and explanations include future rocket ships which will use new propulsion techniques to travel greater distances.

Space Voyagers

http://www.nationalgeographic.com/world/9905/space/index.html

---

Recording Your Space Trip

As Ms. Frizzle and her students were launched into space aboard their *Magic School Bus®*, now a rocket ship, they became astronauts. The first thing they did was to look back at Earth. Their teacher pointed out the blue oceans, white clouds, and brown land of Earth. For the first part of this trip, make a space log for the moon, using the following data.

Moon Data

Diameter: 2,160 miles (3,476 km)
Special Features: no atmosphere, visited by 12 astronauts
Length of Day: 27 days, 7 hours, 43 minutes
Direction of Rotation: west to east (same as Earth's)
Length of year: 365.3 days, same as Earth's
Surface Gravity: .13
Distance from the sun: 93 million miles (149.6 million kilometers), same as Earth's

Become an astronaut and join Ms. Frizzle's class aboard the magic bus/rocket. Experience the adventures her students have as they explore the solar system. Keep a log of what you see and learn, just as other explorers have done. Information about each of the planets you will visit should be recorded in this log. Make copies of the Space Log (page 20) to use for the moon and planets you will visit on this journey. Use a copy of the Space Log to fill in the information about the moon as the first page of your log. Write "Moon" in the blank to indicate this as your location.

The moon moves around Earth in about 28 days and rotates on its axis in about the same length of time. This means we see only one side of the moon from Earth. Demonstrate how this works by walking through the motions of Earth and the moon.

Procedure: Have someone stand still to represent Earth. Pretend you are the moon moving around Earth west to east (counterclockwise). Do this without rotating by always looking in the same direction. The person who is on Earth sees all sides of the moon this way. Now repeat this so the moon turns (rotates) at the same speed as it travels around Earth. This is done by having one side of the moon always facing Earth.

No one knew what the other side of the moon looked like until 1959, when the unmanned Soviet satellite *Luna 3* orbited the moon and took photographs of it. There are many more craters on the other side of the moon. Why are most of the names of these craters Russian?

Internet Extender

Activity Summary: Visit the following Web sites to learn about the moon and Apollo missions. Great pictures and extensive information are available at the first. The second Web site includes detailed information and links to film clips of the *Apollo 11–17* missions.

The Moon

http://spaceart.com/solar/eng/moon.htm

Apollo Missions

http://spaceart.com/solar/eng/apo11.htm

(Reach the other *Apollo* missions by changing *apo11* to *apo12*, etc.)

Space Log

To the Teacher: *Students may need assistance in calculating this information, perhaps by having students work in groups to find the answers. Distribute a copy of the Planet Data chart (page 4) and discuss the information before students use it with their Space Log.*

Entry Date: _____ **Location:** _____

Draw the planet to scale in the box below:

Scale: Earth's Diameter = 5 mm
◯
Earth

Special Features

_____

_____

_____

_____

_____

_____

_____

Use a calculator to help you compute the following data.

Rotation Speed at Equator:

_____ x 3.14 (π) = _____ ÷ _____ = _____
    diameter   circumference at equator   length of day in hours   rotation speed at equator

Direction of Rotation (underline the answer):

west to east (as Earth rotates) or retrograde (opposite direction from the Earth)

My age on this planet:

Mercury – Jupiter: _____ x 365 days = _____ ÷ _____ = _____
                 my age in years   my age in days   planet's year in days   age on this planet

Beyond Jupiter: Would you be 1 year old yet? _____ Would you ever have a birthday here?_____

My weight on this planet:

_____ x _____ = _____
    gravity at surface   my weight   my weight on this planet

Distance from the sun:_____

This planet is the_____ planet from the sun.

Solar System

This diagram of the solar system shows the planets' orbits drawn roughly to scale. If you were able to look down on the solar system, you would see the planets traveling around the sun in a counterclockwise direction. They also travel at different speeds and thus do not travel in a straight path around the sun. All the planets except Pluto travel in about the same plane around the Sun. Pluto's orbit is tilted, relative to the rest of the orbits. The comet orbit is only one example; these orbits are at various angles to the plane of planet orbits.

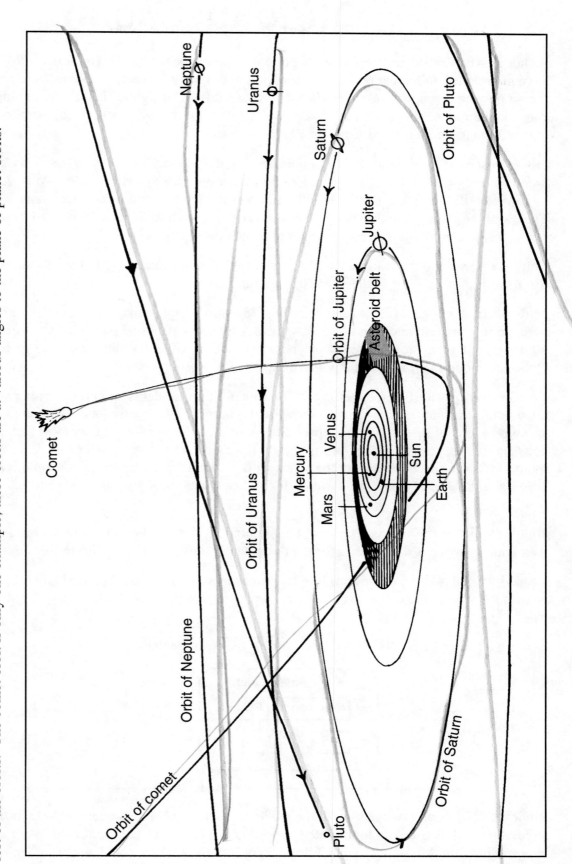

Off to the Moon

Although Ms. Frizzle and her students go to the moon aboard the *Magic School Bus*®, 12 astronauts have gone to the moon using the *Saturn* rocket and *Apollo* spacecraft. Samples of rock and soil from the moon were brought back to Earth for further study. During the final three landings, an electric car was taken along so the astronauts could explore more of the moon's surface. *Apollo 17*, the last of six manned lunar landings, took place in 1972.

Future space exploration may take people back to the moon. Someday, a base may be built on the moon for people to live and work in, much like the one in Antarctica today. At first, this base will only be for scientific research, but eventually mining the moon's natural resources may become possible. The North and South American continents were explored and then developed to make use of their vast resources, eventually leading to the nations which presently exist.

You may be among the astronauts who return to the moon someday. Let's do a simulation of what a trip to visit a moon base in the year 2021 might be like.

Materials: 10 copies of the Moon Transport Mission Script, transparencies of the Lunar Transport Mission information and Lunar route maps, transparency pen, one pair of cloth overalls and work gloves from a paint store, 10 crew patches, four helium-filled balloons, and a large box for the balloon. Optional: moon map, video of *Apollo* missions (See Resource section).

Lesson Preparation: Before setting off on this mission, students should design a crew patch using the crew members' names and pictures showing the purpose of the mission. Show crew patches from space missions of *Apollo* and the Space Shuttle to give ideas of what they look like. These patches can be worn by the crew members during the flight. Decorate the spacesuit (overalls) which will be worn by the Mission Specialist during the space walk to deploy the satellites. It should have a picture of the US flag and NASA symbol (or symbol of another space agency students invent), as well as the mission patch.

Highlight nine scripts for each role of the simulation. Put the helium balloons inside the box. Students may want to make a flight panel for the commander and pilot to use during the simulation.

Procedure: Divide the classroom into five areas as shown below. Set up the overhead projector (ovp) next to the navigator so he/she can mark the progress of the spacecraft during the mission.

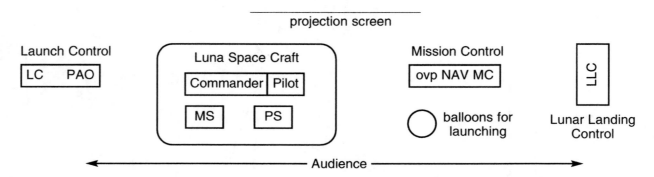

Review the Mission Overview with the students. Select the nine students who will take part in the simulation and distribute a highlighted script to each of them. Let them read over the script before they begin. Show the Mission Specialist how to get into the spacesuit and where to deploy the balloons. Have the remaining students place their seats in the audience area and start the launch.

Lunar Transport Mission

Mission Overview

Space vehicle being launched: Transporter *Luna* carrying four crew members to the moon

Launch site: Kennedy Space Center, Florida

Date of launch: July 20, 2021 (52 years after the first landing on the moon)

Landing site: Sea of Tranquility Moon Base

Length of trip: five days

Crew assignments during mission: Deploy four satellites while in orbit around the moon

Launch Code Words

APU: Auxiliary Power Unit (power unit used before launch)

BFS: Back-Up Flight System (computer)

CSM: Command Service Module (spaceship where crew live during transport to moon)

OPS: Onboard Program System (computer)

T: Time (T minus before launch and T plus after launch)

Ground Controllers

LC: Launch Control (at Kennedy Space Center, controls launch sequence)

LLC: Lunar Landing Control (at Sea of Tranquility on moon, controls landing sequence)

MC: Mission Control (at Houston Space Center, controls mission after launch)

PAO: Public Affairs Officer (announces events of mission to public)

NAV: Navigator (plots progress of flight on maps during the mission)

Crew Members

Commander: Chief pilot in charge of entire flight

Pilot: Second in command of flight

MS: Mission Specialist (in charge of payload development during mission)

PS: Payload Specialist (helps with in-flight mission assignments)

Moon Transport Mission Script

PAO:	It is now T minus 1 hour, 30 minutes, beginning the final countdown for the launch of the space transport *Luna.*
LC:	*Luna,* this is Launch Control radio check.
Commander:	Launch Control, this is *Luna,* we read you loud and clear.
MC:	*Luna,* this is Mission Control radio check.
Commander:	Mission Control, we read you loud and clear.
LC:	*Luna,* ready for abort advisory check.
Pilot:	Roger, abort advisory check is satisfactory.
LC:	*Luna,* this is Launch Control. Side hatch is secure.
Commander:	We copy Launch Control.
MS:	Launch control cabin pressure is fine.
LC:	Roger, we copy.
PS:	Boiler control switch on. Nitrogen supply switch on.
LC:	Roger, we copy.
Pilot:	OMS pressure is on.
MS:	Launch Control, this is *Luna,* cabin vent check complete.
LC:	Roger, *Luna.*
PAO:	The count is at T minus 22 minutes, 16 seconds and holding. This is a planned hold built into the countdown to allow all sequences to be completed before proceeding.
	The navigator will show us the location of the transporter *Luna* on the map. After the launch, the navigator will continue to mark where *Luna* is in space, until it lands on the moon.
☞ *Nav #1:*	(*Mark an X on Lunar Transporter map on #1 position.*)
Commander:	Control, *Luna's* flight plan is loaded into the computer.
LC:	Resume countdown.
Commander:	Control, this is *Luna,* OPS-1 loaded into BFS.
LC:	Roger; we copy.
PAO:	T minus 12 minutes and 29 seconds and counting.
LC:	This is Control, *Luna,* conducting the abort check.
Pilot:	Roger, looks good from here.
PAO:	It is T minus 9 minutes and holding. At this point, there is a scheduled 10 minute hold to allow one last chance to catch up before the final countdown begins.
LC:	It is a go for Launch. Resume countdown.
Commander:	Control, we have activated event timer.
LC:	Roger. Crew access arm is being retracted. Time to initiate APU prestart procedure.
Commander:	Roger. Control prestart complete APUs powered up.
LC:	Roger.
Pilot:	APUs look good.
LC:	This is Control, you are on internal power.

Moon Transport Mission Script *(cont.)*

Commander: Crew, you are go to put your visors down.

Pilot: <u>Launch Control, we have a problem here, the pressure gauge shows a drop in cabin pressure!</u>

LC: Please repeat your message.

Pilot: <u>We have a problem here—the cabin pressure has dropped!</u>

PAO: There is a drop in the cabin pressure of the transport. This sometimes happens when the crew put their visors down and begin to breathe pure oxygen. The countdown will be held until the problem is checked out.

Pilot: <u>Control, this is *Luna* happy to report cabin pressure is OK!</u>

LC: *Luna,* we copy you; the countdown will be resumed.

Commander: Roger, Control.

LC: *Luna,* this is Control. Main engines gimbal complete.

Pilot: Roger, copy that.

LC: *Luna,* this is Control. Oxygen—two vents closed and looking good.

Pilot: Roger.

PAO: We are at T minus 2 minutes, 10 seconds and counting.

LC: You are GO FOR LAUNCH!

Commander: Roger, understand we are GO FOR LAUNCH! We are looking forward to a great flight.

LC: *Luna,* this is Control. APU start is go. Onboard computer switched on.

Commander: Roger.

LC: Beginning the count at 10 seconds, 9, 8, 7, 6, 5, 4, 3, 2 . . . 1 . . . zero—LIFTOFF!

☞ *Nav #2* *(Draw line on map to #2 location.)*

PAO: We have liftoff of the space transport *Luna.* Go, baby, go!

Great storms of burning fuel, orange and red in the gray-black smoke, are billowing out of the rocket. There are 50,000 gallons of water a minute being dumped on the launch site to cool it and keep down exhaust fumes.

LC: All engines are looking good. Instituting maneuver for orbit angle. Orbit maneuver completed, *Luna;* you look good.

☞ *Nav #3* *(Draw line on map to #3 location.)*

Commander: Control, this is *Luna.* Beginning roll program.

PAO: Onboard guidance systems are now tipping the *Luna* slightly to fly southeast over the Atlantic. We now transfer to Houston for Mission Control to take over the mission.

MC: Roger, we are 1 minute and 11 seconds into the flight.

Commander: Control, this is *Luna;* roll completed and pitch is programmed.

MC: Roger, we copy. Thrust is go all engines.

Commander: Roger, full thrust all engines. First stage is now falling away. Second stage firing. Mission Control, <u>we are in orbit!</u>

Moon Transport Mission Script *(cont.)*

☞   ***Nav #4***   *(Draw line on map to #4 location.)*

MC: Roger, we copy, it is T plus 12 minutes, orbit has been achieved. Throttle back and release second stage.

Pilot: Mission Control, this is *Luna,* we have throttled back, second stage is away. Orbit speed is 17,500 miles per hour.

MC: Roger, we copy that.

PAO: The transporter will be parked in an orbit 120 miles above Earth until it is time to fire the third stage rocket to send it toward the moon.

MC: This is Mission Control, *Luna.* Check systems in CSM and third stage rocket.

☞   ***Nav #5***   *(Change map to one showing earth and moon. Mark an X on position #5.)*

Commander: Roger, CSM systems and rocket check OK.

MC: This is Mission Control, third stage rocket ignition at 5 . . . 4 . . . 3 . . . 2 . . .1—Fire!

Pilot: Ignition is successful. <u>WOW, what a kick!</u> Our speed is now 24,400 miles per hour!

☞   ***Nav #6***   *(Draw a line to position #6.)*

Commander: We are leaving Earth's orbit and heading toward the moon.

Pilot: Third stage away, we will float toward the moon now.

MC: Roger. Good luck on your 225,000 mile journey.

PAUSE

☞   ***Nav #7***   *(Draw a line to position #7.)*

PAO: It is two days after the launch, and the transporter is being slowed by the pull of Earth's gravity.

Commander: Mission Control, this is *Luna,* our speed is now 2,300 miles per hour.

MC: Roger. You will soon be picked up by the moon's gravity.

PAUSE

☞   ***Nav #8***   *(Draw a line to position #8.)*

PAO: Three days have passed since the launch at Kennedy Space Center.

Pilot: Control, we are feeling the pull of the moon, and it is increasing our speed.

MC: Prepare to fire service module engines as you come around the moon.

PAO: This burn will take place on the back side of the moon. Since no communication can pass through the moon to Earth, the commander will control the countdown. Only after *Luna* has come from behind the moon will we know if the engines fired successfully.

Moon Transport Mission Script *(cont.)*

☞ *Nav #9* *(Draw a line to position #9.)*

Pilot: Engines fired on time, and we are in orbit around the moon!

☞ *Nav #10* *(Draw a line to position #10.)*

PAO: At this time, the payload specialist assists the mission specialist into the spacesuit to leave the transport and deploy a series of satellites which will orbit the moon, making it possible to communicate with all areas of the moon. The mission specialist moves through the airlock and steps out into the emptiness of space. A thin line keeps the astronaut from floating away.

PS: How are you doing out there?

MS: I feel great! The view is <u>magnificent.</u> The earth looks like a small blue marble from here; the moon is enormous. Oh look at that! I can see the moon base below me!

☞ *Nav #11* *(Draw a line to position #11.)*

PS: You're right; that is a spectacular view! Prepare to deploy satellites. Don't ruin them—remember they cost millions of dollars!

MS: Don't worry, I wouldn't ruin them. Deploying satellites now. (Open the box and release the four helium balloons, one at a time.)

☞ *Nav #12* *(Draw a line to position #12.)*

PS: Satellites look good from here. Data readings are good. You can float around out there and enjoy the scenery for awhile. Don't forget to keep your line hooked to the transporter.

Pilot: Looks like he's really enjoying himself out there. Don't float away too far; it's a long way home from here.

PAUSE

☞ *Nav #13* *(Draw a line to position #13.)*

PS: Time to come back inside and prepare for lunar landing.

☞ *Nav #14* *(Draw a line to position #14.)*

PAO: The crew of *Luna* has been in orbit for one day around the moon and is now preparing to land at the Sea of Tranquility Moon Base.

Commander: All crew members return to your seats and prepare for retrorocket burn. Lunar Landing Control, this is *Luna*. Retrorocket burn complete.

☞ *Nav #15* *(Draw a line to position #15.)*

LLC: Roger, we copy. We'll be glad to have you join us at the moon base. Call out your altitude as you near landing.

Pilot: We are at 500 feet, 400 . . . 300 . . . 200 . . . 100

☞ *Nav #16* *(Draw a line to position #16.)*

Commander: Landing gear down and locked.

Pilot: <u>Contact, *Luna* has landed!</u>

LLC: <u>Welcome to the Sea of Tranquility Moon Base!</u>

☞ *Nav #17* *(Draw a line to position #17.)*

PAO: The transporter *Luna* has made a successful landing on the moon. The crew will now transfer to the base and begin their work on the moon.

Route of the Lunar Transport *Luna* Part 1

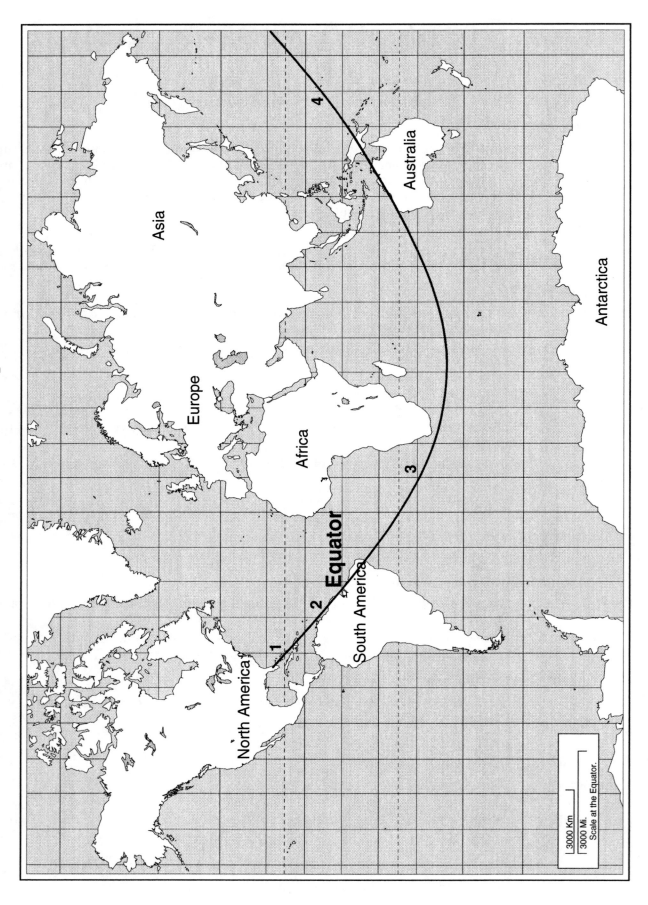

Route of the Lunar Transport *Luna* Part 2

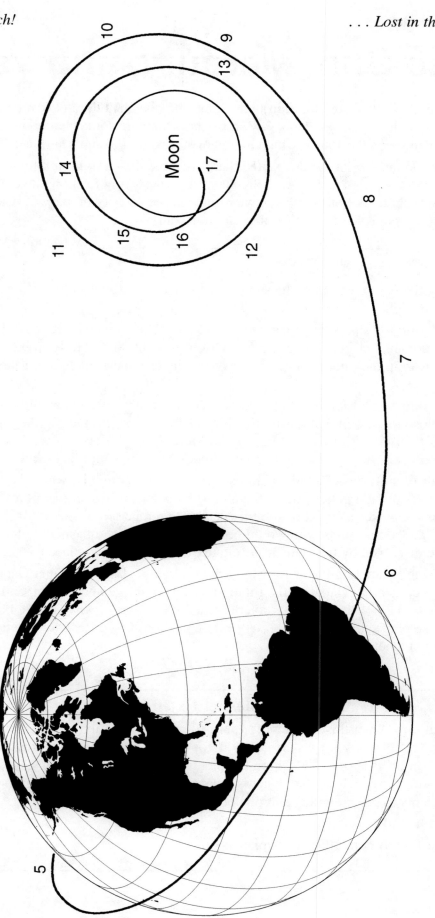

The Sun, Mercury, and Venus

The bus zoomed toward the sun but didn't stay long. It was much too hot (over 11,000° F or 6,093° C) and dangerous to look at. The students saw sunspots, which are somewhat cooler spots on the sun's surface. They also saw solar flares, which are giant storms on the sun's surface.

Gregory's report on the size of the sun stated that it is more than a million kilometers across. The sun is about 870,000 miles (1,392,000 km) in diameter. Use the string to show the diameter of the sun compared to the scale model of the planets you made in the activity on page 7. Calculate the length of this string using the same scale (Earth's diameter = 10 cm).

_____ ÷ _____ = _____ x 10 cm = _____
Diameter of the sun   Earth's diameter   length of string for model

After measuring the string, compare the sun's size to that of the planets by holding the string along the top of the scale model.

Carmen's report said the sun is an "average star. There are stars which are much bigger than the sun. Betelgeuse, a red giant star in the constellation Orion, is 433,000,000 miles (692.8 million km) in diameter! If it were in the middle of our solar system, every planet including Mars would be *inside the star.*

Next, the bus zoomed past Mercury and Venus. Neither of these planets would be a good place to live. Mercury is so close to the sun that during the day, lead would melt. During the night on Mercury, it would be colder than liquid nitrogen. One day on Mercury is 59 Earth days long. It rotates very slowly, as you will see when you complete your Space Log entry on this planet.

Venus has clouds of sulfuric acid and an atmosphere of carbon dioxide, which is 91 times heavier than that on Earth. The sunlight is trapped by the atmosphere, so surface temperatures are extremely hot, like being inside a closed car on a hot summer day. The temperature is over 900° F (482° C) on the surface. If you landed on Venus, you would be baked by its heat, squashed by the weight of its atmosphere, and dissolved by the acids in its clouds! It is not a good place to take a vacation!

Closure: Complete Space Log pages for Mercury and Venus. Use the Planet Data (page 4) chart to get the information you need to calculate the rotation speed, your age and weight, and other statistics. Notice how slowly both of these planets rotate compared to Earth. Also, notice how much older you would be on these planets than on Earth. Use reference books (see Resource section) to find special features about the planets for your log.

Internet Extender

Activity Summary: Visit this Web site for easy-to-read information which shows the location for each planet in the solar system, its size, how it got its name, number of moons, what it is made of and a description of its surface. Click on the pictures to enlarge the view. Click on sky map (except for Earth) to see where the planet is located in the sky for the present month. Assign groups of students to research different planets and report to the class.

The Planets for Kids

http://www.dustbunny.com/afk/planets/planets.htm

Welcome to Mars

To the Teacher: *See the Resource section of this book for a Mars map and video.*

Ahhh, this planet is much better than the others we have just visited. Ms. Frizzle and her class discovered that Mars has two moons, neither of which are spheres like Earth's moon. The reason for this was explained in John's report. He said the moons were too small to have enough gravity to form them into a round ball.

The students also saw that Mars has ice caps at the poles, just like those on Earth. The canyon Valles Marineris on Mars is 3,000 miles (4,800 km) long, running just south of the equator. This canyon would stretch all the way across the United States. The Grand Canyon would be a mere ditch by comparison! Olympus Mons, a volcano on Mars, is the largest in the solar system. It is 16.8 miles (27 km) high and would cover the state of Oregon. Even the great Hawaiian volcano Mauna Kea, which is 6.8 miles (10 km) high from the ocean floor to its top, is dwarfed by Olympus Mons. Surface features of dry river valleys and flood zones on Mars show that there was once water flowing there. Today, most of that water is frozen in the ice caps and soil. Mars' soil is red, mainly because it contains so much iron. The moisture in Mars' atmosphere turns the iron to rust.

There are great wind storms on Mars, especially near the polar caps. Dust from soil picked up by winds makes the sky pink on this planet. Like Earth, Mars has seasons; in the spring the polar caps shrink, and dark surface markings spread toward the equator. In fall, the caps begin to increase as the temperatures cool off and the markings fade. These markings may be sand storms. Temperature ranges on Mars are 72° F to –194° F (22° C to –125° C) compared to Earth's 136° F to –127° F (58° C to –88° C).

Mars has been visited by two satellites, *Viking I* and *Viking II*, which landed on Mars in 1976 in two different locations. The information they sent back through pictures and measurements of temperature, atmospheric conditions, and soil content has encouraged scientists to think seriously about exploring this planet. There are plans to send more satellites and unmanned landers to Mars, in preparation for a manned mission to this planet. You may be a crew member on the first flight to Mars.

Closure: Complete a Space Log page for Mars and notice how light you would be on that planet. This would make moving around much easier. You would still need a spacesuit to protect yourself from temperature extremes and provide the oxygen you need, since the Martian atmosphere is mostly carbon dioxide. Although the length of day on Mars is about the same number of hours as on Earth, Mars rotates only about half as fast as Earth. Can you explain that? (Hint: Think about the size of Mars compared to Earth.)

Internet Extender

Activity Summary: Relive the 1997 landing on Mars. The information here covers the history of the mission, animated views, and images such as "Many Rovers" showing composite panoramic views of the rover and lander on Mars' surface.

Mars Pathfinder

http://spaceart.com/solar/eng/path.htm

Pathfinder Images

http://spaceart.com/solar/cap/path/index.htm

Mars Data

Remember the activity you did earlier to draw the planets' orbits (page 11)? You discovered that Mars' orbit was offset from that of Earth; thus, there are times when the two planets are closer together. Let's do an activity to see how this looks if you were observing Mars and Earth from a distance out in space. The orbits of these planets are shown below, illustrating the months of the year on Earth's orbit and the corresponding positions on Mars' orbit. Enlarge the drawing of these orbits and connect the planets for the first six months. The first position is done.

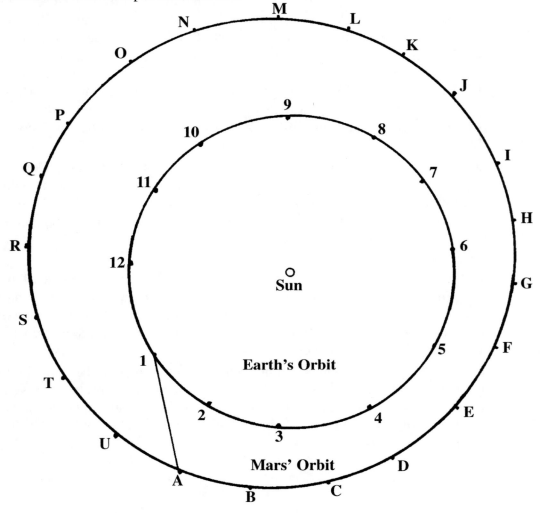

Where are Earth and Mars the closest? #_____ and letter _____

Continue to connect the positions between Earth and Mars for one Earth year. Where was Mars most distant from Earth? #_____ and letter _____

How would the view of Mars from Earth be different from the closest and the most distant positions?

_____

Why are there more positions shown on Mars' orbit than on Earth's orbit?

_____

To see an interesting pattern, connect the positions between Mars and Earth for five Earth years.

Jupiter

As the Magic Bus passed through the Asteroid Belt, one of the asteroids struck a taillight and broke it. Ms. Frizzle put on a spacesuit and went out to repair the light. Suddenly, another asteroid passed by and cut her tether line, setting her adrift from the bus. The class and bus zoomed off, with Janet coming to the rescue by finding Ms. Frizzle's lesson book in the glove compartment and serving as narrator. The bus moved closer to the largest planet, Jupiter.

Look at the scale model of the planets you did in an earlier lesson (page 7) and review the comparison of the size of Jupiter with that of Earth. The huge red spot on this planet, as large as three Earths, is a storm which has been raging for at least 300 years. The winds in this storm are 225 mph (360 km per hour)! Jupiter has a ring around it which is too faint to be easily seen from Earth.

Complete a Space Log page for Jupiter. Notice that this giant planet rotates at 28,061 mph (44,897 kph)! For comparison, a commercial jet flies at about 580 mph (928 kph). The fastest jet is the Air Force's Blackbird at 2,000 mph (3,200 kph), and the Space Shuttle orbits the Earth at about 17,500 mph (28,000 kph). None of these moves even half as fast as Jupiter rotates!

Jupiter's Moons

The Father of Astronomy, Galileo Galilei, was the first person to look at our moon and the planets through a telescope in 1610. He kept a notebook with drawings of what he observed. Look carefully at the drawings of his sketches of Jupiter's moons made during 15 observations.

Jupiter's Moons as Recorded by Galileo in 1610

Key: ◯ = Jupiter   ○ = moon

In 1610, most people thought that everything in space, including the planets and the sun, orbited the Earth. Galileo used his observations to prove that Jupiter had moons and they were orbiting Jupiter, not the Earth.

What was the greatest number of moons he saw during his observations? _____

How do his drawings prove the moons orbited around Jupiter? _____

_____

Saturn, Uranus, and Neptune

The next planet to come into view was Saturn, with its magnificent rings. These rings were first seen by Galileo in 1610 when he observed the planet and wrote that he observed "ears" on it. His telescope was not good enough to make out the rings. They also turned edge-on to Earth during part of the time he observed them and could not be seen. Galileo never knew he had really seen rings around this planet. Another astronomer, Christian Huygens, using a better telescope in 1656, was able to see the rings. The rings are made up of rock, ice, and dust. Scientists think this may be a moon of Saturn which got too close to the planet and was torn apart by its tremendous gravitational pull or perhaps pieces of material which never pulled together to form a moon.

Uranus, a lovely blue-green giant planet, was the next planet the students visited. It also had rings but looked very strange since it is tipped on its side. *Voyager 2,* an unmanned satellite, flew by Uranus in January 1986 and sent back pictures of the planet and its moons. Scientists looked at the scars on the moons of Uranus and developed a theory that a comet or asteroid passed near the planet long ago. Its gravitational pull may have broken apart one of the moons which later pulled back together. This same pull of gravity may have tipped Uranus on its side. The axis of Uranus is always tipped in the same direction, which turns different hemispheres to the sunlight during its 84-year journey around the sun.

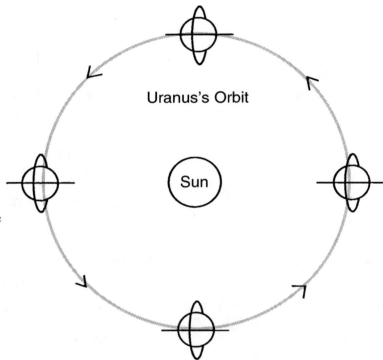

The bus was going faster and faster as it swept by Neptune. This planet, almost the same size as Uranus, is a blue giant. It has storms in its atmosphere and, like Jupiter, a great dark spot which is also a storm. Neptune has rings around it just like all the other giant planets. Remember the drawing you did of the planets' orbits (page 12) which showed that Neptune's orbit is sometimes inside that of Pluto. Neptune was for a period of time the most distant planet from the sun until 1999.

Closure: Make Space Log pages for Saturn, Uranus, and Neptune. Compare the rotation speeds of these four planets and your weight on them in the next lesson.

Internet Extender

Activity Summary: Scan down to Browse the Galileo Gallery of Io Images to take a tour on the Galileo satellite as it passes Jupiter and Io. Film clips show Jupiter and its moon, Io, as well as a volcanic plume rising from Io's surface.

Galileo Satellite Visits Jupiter

http://galileo.jpl.nasa.gov/

Comparing the Giant Planets

Complete the following chart, using your Space Logs and the Planet Data chart. The information for the Earth has been added for you, except for your weight.

Data	Earth	Jupiter	Saturn	Uranus	Neptune
Surface Gravity	1.00 g				
Your Weight on . . .					
Diameter Relative to Earth's	1.00				
Rotation Speed at Equator	1,043 mph (1,669 kph)				

On which of these giant planets would you be lighter than on Earth?_____

Did you notice that although these planets are much larger than Earth, you really don't appear to weigh much more than you do on Earth? This is because you are calculating your weight at the "surface" of the atmosphere of these giant planets. These huge planets are mostly made of gas which becomes denser as you move toward the center. At the top of the atmosphere, you are very far from the most massive part of the planet, which is located at its center. The more mass, the more gravity. So, the further you are from the mass, the less gravity can pull on you and therefore you get lighter. This can be compared to moving away from Earth. The higher you get above Earth, the less you weigh until you gradually become weightless (as in the Space Shuttle).

Earth's rotation moves the atmosphere around. This can be seen from space by watching the clouds in the atmosphere. Pictures sent back to Earth from *Voyager 1* and *2* showed raging storms moving swiftly in the atmospheres of all the giant planets. Use the information from the chart about the rotation speeds of the four giants to explain the storms on these planets.

_____

_____

_____

Closure: The pictures from the *Voyager* satellites showed that all the giant planets have rings around their equators. The rings around Jupiter are very faint. Those around Uranus are tipped almost 90 degrees, as its equator is tipped. Add rings to the four giant planets in the scale models you made earlier (page 7), and to the drawings in your Space Logs for these planets.

Mark the progress of the bus on the Planets' Orbits on the chart in your Space Log, as well as the large chart made earlier (page 12).

Pluto: God of the Underworld

The bus was traveling so fast it nearly missed the ninth planet, Pluto, and its moon, Charon. Pluto was tiny and dark since the sun was only a bright star, very far away. Wanda's report said that scientists once thought Pluto was an escaped moon of Neptune. It is still not certain what Pluto is. Some scientists think it may be entirely made of ice.

The planets Uranus, Neptune, and Pluto were discovered after telescopes were invented because they are so far away and therefore too small to see. Uranus was discovered by William Herschel in 1781, using a telescope he built himself. The newly discovered planet appeared to speed up and slow down in its orbit, as if something were tugging on it. This suggested that there might be another nearby planet pulling it. A young English astronomer, John Adams, began to search for that nearby planet, and a French mathematician, Urbain Leverrier, worked out the orbit to show where it would be located. The planet Neptune was discovered in 1846, and both men were given credit for finding it.

Some scientists thought there might be a ninth planet, nicknamed *Planet X*. Percival Lowell, a wealthy person who loved astronomy, built an observatory in Flagstaff, Arizona, to search for Planet X and to study Mars. He died before the ninth planet, Pluto, was discovered, but it was found by using the telescope at his observatory. A young observatory assistant, Clyde Tambaugh, found Pluto in 1930. The name *Pluto*, the Roman god of the underworld, was suggested by an 11-year-old English girl since the planet was so far away and completely dark.

Pluto's tiny moon, Charon, was not discovered until 1978. A photograph of Pluto, taken through a telescope, was enlarged 80 times and showed that the planet had a bulge on it. Astronomers realized the bulge must be a moon close to Pluto. Since the moon is not much smaller than Pluto, they move like two twirling dancers.

The Dance of Pluto and Charon

Let's simulate the way Pluto and Charon move in their dance. Have a large person be Pluto and a smaller one be Charon. They face each other and hold hands. The one who is Pluto begins to rotate, taking Charon with him or her so they turn together.

Closure: Write a Space Log for the last planet. One complete spin of Pluto and Charon takes a day. Look at your Space Log to find the length of a day on Pluto. Is this a slow or fast dance?

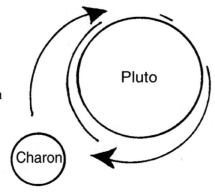

Internet Extender

Activity Summary: Visit the Web site to learn the latest information about Pluto. View the pictures, which can be enlarged, and follow links to animated views of Pluto and its moon Charon.

Pluto

http://spaceart.com/solar/eng/pluto.htm

Where Is Planet X?

When Clyde Tambaugh searched for Pluto, he used a "blink" machine which blinked between two pictures taken of the same section of sky a few nights apart. He was searching for any star that appeared to move back and forth during the blinking process. Only planets, asteroids, and comets move in the sky within the time period of a few nights. The stars stay in the same position.

Astronomers knew that planets closely follow the same path the sun takes across the sky, as shown on the Solar System chart (page 21). The planets and sun appear to be on the same plane, except for Pluto, which has an orbit that is slightly tipped to all the other orbits. Many pictures were taken of the area where it was thought Pluto might be found. It took months of looking at these photographs during the search for Pluto. Let's do an activity which shows what this search was like.

The two drawings below simulate photographs of the same star field made on different nights. Can you find one star which changes its position? Use a plain piece of paper to help you examine the two pictures by slowly pulling it down the pictures as you scan across the top edge of it. Look for a change in the pattern of the dots between pictures #1 and #2 to find the one which has moved. Draw a circle around it.

Closure: If you could put these pictures on the blink machine used by Clyde Tambaugh, that dot would appear to jump from one position to the other as the two pictures are quickly viewed back and forth. This is slow, tedious work and takes a lot of patience. This same technique is used today to find asteroids and comets.

Planets on the Move

When you wrote your Space Log about Pluto, you discovered that it takes 248 Earth years for the planet to move once around the sun. Compare this with the length of Mercury's year, and you will see a big difference in their speed.

(1) Scientists think the solar system formed some 4.6 billion years ago as a vast cloud of gas and dust. This cloud may have been shaken by a nearby exploding star, making it collapse into a spinning disk.

(2) Gravitation pulled so much material to the center that pressure and heat there lit a nuclear fire: the sun began to shine.

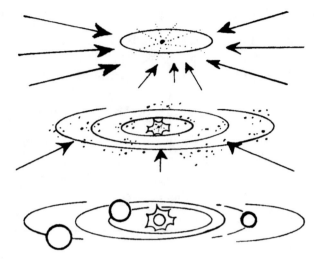

(3) Other material continued to revolve around the sun and slowly collected into lumps of hot solids and gases, which cooled into planets. The closer a planet is to the sun, the faster it moves in its orbit around the Sun.

Let's do an activity to stimulate the motion of the planets at various distances from the sun.

Materials: half a drinking straw, 2 feet (60 cm) of light string, two large rubber washers

Procedure: Put the string through the straw and tie a washer to each end. Hold the straw high above your head and begin spinning the string so that one washer will go out as far as possible. Once the string is spinning, hold your hand still and slowly pull down on the other washer, shortening the string on the spinning washer. Watch the speed of the washer as it moves closer to the straw.

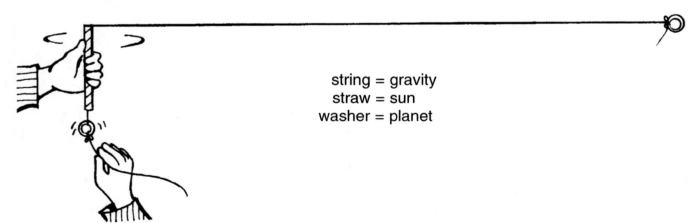

string = gravity
straw = sun
washer = planet

Closure: The straw represents the sun, and the string is its gravity which pulls on the planet (washer). So long as the planet remains in motion, it continues to orbit the sun. The planet goes faster as it gets closer to the sun. This same motion exists between a planet and its moon, or any satellite in orbit around it.

What would happen if the planets suddenly stopped revolving around the sun? To find this answer, spin the planet (washer) again, then stop spinning. Watch what happens to the planet.

Comets

The solar system contains the sun, planets and their moons, asteroids, and comets. For a long time, people had no idea where comets came from, and many thought they brought wars and disease. Sir Edmund Halley, a British astronomer, in 1705 made a study of records of comet sightings and was able to calculate their orbits. He noticed that three comets sighted in 1531, 1607, and 1682 had orbits which were nearly the same size, shape, and location in space. He thought these could all be the same comet which returned about every 75 years. He predicted it would reappear in 1758–1759. Although he did not live to see it, the comet returned on Christmas Day, 1758, and was given Halley's name in his honor. This famous comet has passed through Earth's orbit in 1836, 1910, and 1985. In 1910 it came so close that our planet actually passed through the tail of the comet. It will pass this way again in 2061.

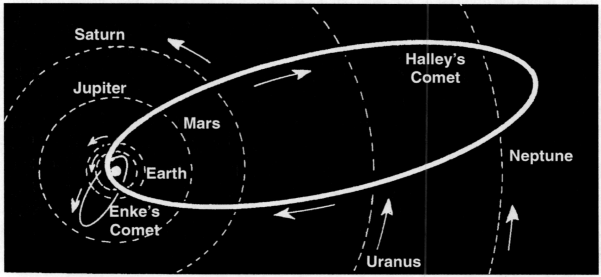

There are billions of comets; most seem to come from an area about 45,000 times farther from the sun than Earth. This cluster of comets is called the "Oort Cloud," after the Dutch astronomer who suggested that an area exists where the leftover material from the solar system formed this cloud. A passing star's gravity can fling a comet into a cigar-shaped orbit that brings it close to the sun.

Jupiter was struck by a comet which broke apart as it neared the planet in July, 1994. Twenty one large fragments and many smaller ones from the comet plowed into the clouds of the giant planet, leaving dark scars which could be seen through telescopes on Earth.

The length of time for a comet to pass by the sun, called its *period*, depends upon the size of its orbit. Some comets have a short period, such as Encke which reappears every 3.3 years, while others may take thousands of years or only appear once. Comet orbits can go beyond Pluto's or closer to the sun than Jupiter's orbit.

Internet Extender

Activity Summary: Learn about Comet Halley and see pictures of it taken by the satellite Giotto at the first Web site below. The second one has pictures of the spectacular collision of a comet with Jupiter in 1994.

Comet Halley

http://spaceart.com/solar/eng/halley.htm

Comet Shoemaker-Levy Home Page

http://www.jpl.nasa.gov/s19/

Making a Comet

Astronomer Dr. Fred Whipple called comets "dirty snowballs." Let's make a comet and see what one would look like.

Materials: 2 cups (250 mL) water, ammonia, 2 spoonfuls of sand, 10 pounds (4.5 kg) dry ice, large bowl or tray, hammer, gloves, large wooden or metal spoon

(*Note:* Dry ice may be purchased from ice cream shops. It is extremely cold and should be handled with gloves. It evaporates rapidly and should be used soon after purchase. If it is to be stored for a few hours, wrap it in layers of paper and store it in an ice chest, not a freezer.)

Procedure: Break the dry ice into pieces about the size of a golf ball. Pour the water, a few drops of ammonia, and sand into the bowl and mix these with the large spoon. These represent the hydrogen, oxygen, ammonia, and dirt found in the comet nucleus. Next, mix in the largest ingredient of the nucleus, dry ice, which is frozen carbon dioxide. At this point carbon dioxide gas will be given off as the dry ice begins to warm and evaporate. The gas is heavier than atmospheric gases and thus begins to roll down toward the floor. This gas is harmless in a room where fresh air is free to enter and provide oxygen to breathe.

Parts of a Comet

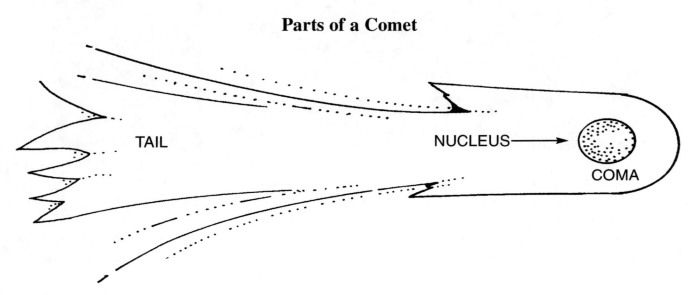

TAIL   NUCLEUS——→   COMA

The gas escaping from the nucleus of the comet creates the coma and tail which only become visible as a comet passes near the sun and heats up. The tail may be 600,000 to 60 million miles long (1 million to 100 million km). It is always pushed away from the comet by the sun's radiation, even when the comet is moving away from the sun. Listen to the sounds your comet makes. It pops and whistles as it evaporates, just like a real comet would. Jets of gas escaping make the comet tumble as it travels in its orbit. It also loses pieces of its nucleus as it melts, leaving them in its path across the orbits of the planets. When Earth passes through these areas of comet dust in its orbit, gravity pulls some of it into our atmosphere. Friction from the air burns up the dust, leaving a bright flash and sometimes even a streak if the chunk is large. These are called meteors. Meteor showers can be predicted since Earth revisits these same areas of deposits in its orbit every year.

Closure: Blow on your comet to simulate the heat of the sun and watch the tail rush away from you. Give your comet a name and place it where it can be observed as it evaporates.

Vacation in Space

To the Students: Now that you have toured the solar system, pick your favorite planet or the moon that you visited and put together a travel brochure and display that will make people want to take a vacation trip to that location. Use your Space Log, data charts, books, and magazines to help you gather information for your project. Your project should include the following:

 ✧ A colorful travel brochure describing the special features of this vacation spot. Include pictures of the spacecraft used to transport the tourists. Show the cabins, dining and recreation areas on board. Be sure to include the prices for passengers traveling first class or economy. Get brochures from a travel agency to see how they describe cruises and trips to various vacation spots such as Hawaii, Europe, and Antarctica.

 ✧ A three-dimensional representation of the planet or moon they will visit, constructed from a Styrofoam ball. Paint it and show some of the surface features, such as craters, mountains, and polar ice caps. If the planet has moons or rings, be sure to attach these to your model.

 ✧ A map to show where the planet or moon is located in the solar system and what route would be followed from Earth to get there. Use NASA's Exploration of the Solar System chart (page 42) to help calculate how long it takes to make the trip. Use reference books to find the path these satellites used to get to the planets or that the Apollo spacecraft used to get to the moon.

 ✧ A shoebox diorama showing what people will wear and where they will stay when they arrive. Show the sky and any moons which may be visible. If the planet is one of the giant gas planets, people may stay aboard an orbiting space station and make short trips to the moons and rings of these planets.

Remember that you need to interest the tourists in buying the tickets on this vacation trip, so be sure to give as much information as you can to persuade them to go.

Internet Extender

Activity Summary: Have the students visit this Web site and select a spectacular astronomical postcard to send someone via e-mail.

Postcards from Space

http://www.dustbunny.com/afk/postcards/postcards.htm

NASA's Exploration of the Solar System

This information was taken from the NASA Information Summaries, PMS 010-A (JPL) June, 1991, "Our Solar System at a Glance." Teachers may order a copy of the summary from the Jet Propulsion Laboratory (see Resources).

Spacecraft	Mission	Launched	Arrived
Mariner 2	Venus flyby	8/14/62	12/14/62
Mariner 4	Mars flyby	11/28/64	7/14/65
Mariner 5	Venus flyby	6/14/67	10/19/67
Mariner 6	Mars flyby	2/24/69	7/31/69
Mariner 7	Mars flyby	3/27/69	8/5/69
Apollo 11	Land two astronauts on moon	7/16/69	7/20/69
Mariner 9	Orbited Mars	5/30/71	11/18/71
Pioneer 10	Jupiter flyby	3/2/72	12/3/73
Pioneer 11	Jupiter/Saturn flyby	4/5/73	12/2/74 (Jupiter) 9/1/79 (Saturn)
Mariner 10	Venus/Mercury flybys	11/3/73	2/5/74 (Venus) 3/29/74 (Mercury)
Viking 1	Unmanned landing on Mars	8/20/75	7/19/76 (in orbit) 7/20/76 (landing)
Viking 2	Unmanned landing	9/9/75	8/7/76 (in orbit) 9/3/76 (landing)
Voyager 1	Tour of Jupiter	9/5/77	3/7/79 (Jupiter) 11/12/80 (Saturn)
Voyager 2	Tour of outer planets	8/20/77	7/9/79 (Jupiter) 8/25/81 (Saturn) 1/24/86 (Uranus) 8/25/89 (Neptune)
Pioneer Venus 1	Orbit Venus	5/20/78	12/4/78
Pioneer Venus 2	Venus, land probes	8/8/78	12/9/79
Magellan	Venus orbit and mapping	5/5/89	8/10/90
Galileo	Jupiter, drop probes	10/18/89	12/7/95

Apollo spacecraft were the only manned missions to the moon. There were six landings in all.
Note: No satellites have visited Pluto, but this trip would take at least 14 years.

The length of the trip depends upon where the planet is relative to Earth at launch time. When using this data to find how long the trip is to a planet, take the average of the trips listed. Unlike the *Magic School Bus*®, spacecraft launched from Earth do not travel in a straight path to the moon or planets. Sometimes they use another planet to boost their speed to get to their destination.

Related Books and Periodicals

Collins, Michael. "Mission to Mars." *National Geographic*, November 1988. This outstanding article, written by the astronaut who piloted the command module on the *Apollo 11* mission to the moon, describes a future mission to Mars. The article includes drawings and photographs of the mission, including astronaut training, the spaceship and route, and Mars Base 2050.

Dickinson, Terence. *Exploring the Night Sky.* Firefly Books, PO Box 1338, Ellicott Station, Buffalo, NY 14025, 1987. This is an award-winning children's book which takes a step-by-step cosmic voyage from Earth to a distance of 300 million light years, as well as detailed investigations of the planets and information about observing constellations.

Gallant, Roy A. *Our Universe.* National Geographic Society, 1994. This is filled with outstanding illustrations and photographs of the sun and planets. The text is easy to read and very informative.

Kluger, Jeffrey. "Uncovering the Secrets of Mars," *Time*, July 14, 1997. Here are outstanding text, photographs, and diagrams depicting the launch and landing of the Mars *Pathfinder*. The colored photos on the cover and within the article are 3-D images of the Sojourner and landing site. (Back issues may be ordered from Time: 800-843 TIME.)

Mammana, Dennis. *The Night Sky.* Running Press, 1989. This book provides interesting and easy-to-do investigations and observations of the constellations, planets, moon , and stars.

Sagan, Carl. *Cosmos.* Random House, 1980. This is an excellent book for the non-scientists, providing updated and historical information on the topic of astronomy.

Sneider, Cary I. *Earth, Moon, and Stars*, 1986. Great Explorations in Math and Science (GEMS), Lawrence Hall of Science. Order from NSTA; see Materials section. This teacher's guide includes activities related to early concepts of astronomy, Earth's shape and gravity, moon phases and eclipses, and star maps.

Young, Greg. *Exploring Mars: Challenging.* (TCM 2383) Teacher Created Materials, Inc., 1997. (800) 662-4321. This is a teacher's guide of hands-on activities related to the Mars *Pathfinder* and Mars *Global Surveyor* missions (grades 5–7). Activities include making a time line of space exploration and understanding orbits.

_____*Exploring Mars: Intermediate.* (TCM 2383) Teacher Created Materials, Inc., 1997. (800) 662-4321. This is a teacher's guide of hands-on activities related to the Mars Pathfinder and Mars Global Surveyor missions (grades 3–5). These include creating a string design of the orbits of Mars and Earth, retrograde motion, and identifying rocks and minerals.

Young, Ruth M. *Science Simulations: Challenging* (TCM 2107) Teacher Created Materials, Inc., 1997. (800) 662-4321. Simulations include a trip to Mars in the year 2025, as well as communicating with intelligent life beyond our solar system (grades 5–7).

_____*Exploring Mars: Primary.* (TCM 2381) Teacher Created Materials Inc., 1997. (800) 662-4321. Hands-on activities include building a model of the Rover and a play depicting the Rover's trip to Mars. (for students in grades 2–4)

Related Books and Materials *(cont.)*

Sutton, Debra, et al., *Moons of Jupiter,* 1993. Great Explorations in Math and Science (GEMS), Lawrence Hall of Science. Order from NSTA; see Materials Section. Activities for grades 4–9 to investigate a study of Jupiter's moons.

Van Cleave, Janice. *Astronomy for Every Kid.* John Wiley & Sons, 1991. Included are activities and projects with a list of materials, instructions, expected results, and explanations.

Young, Ruth, M. *Space: Intermediate.* Teacher Created Materials, Inc., 1994. This teacher's guide includes hands-on activities related to the solar system, moon, and space travel.

Related Materials

Astronomical Society of the Pacific. 390 Ashton Ave., San Francisco, CA 94112, (800)335-2624. Request a free catalog showing a wide selection of materials related to astronomy, including slides, posters, videos, and computer software. Teachers are also eligible to receive free copies of *The Universe in the Classroom,* a quarterly newsletter produced by ASP.

Carolina Biological Supply Co., 2700 York Rd., Burlington, NC 27215. (800)334-5551. Supplies science materials, including astronomy videos, books, games, charts, and kits.

CORE (NASA's Central Operation of Resources for Educators), Lovain County JVS, 15181 Route 28 South, Oberlin, OH 44074 (216)774-1051, Ext. 293 or 294. Provides materials from NASA to use with students, including: slides, videos, and photographs taken from satellites and space missions to the moon and from the Space Shuttle, as well as curriculum materials.

Delta Education, PO Box 3000, Nashua, NH 03071-3000 (800)442-5444. Supplies science materials including solar system mobile, videos, and astronomical hands-on kit and guide.

Edmund Scientific Co., 101 East Gloucester Pike, Barrington, NJ 08007-1380 (609)547-8880. Supplies aids for teaching astronomy, including telescopes, globes, murals, books, and posters.

Jet Propulsion Laboratory, Teaching Resource Center, Mail Stop CS-530, 4800 Oak Grove Dr., Pasadena, CA 91009. Supplies videotapes of "JPL Computer Graphics," including the five-minute long "Mars the Movie". Also offers photographs and videos of the planets taken by various satellites such as *Voyagers I* and *II*, and videotapes on *Apollo*, Space Shuttle, and *Voyager.*

National Geographic Society, PO Box 2118, Washington, DC 20013-2118 (800)447-0647. Supplies maps and posters such as The Heavens, The Earth's Moon, Solar System/Celestial Family, and The Universe. Back issues of *National Geographic* may be ordered. Call to receive a free catalog.

National Science Teachers Association (NSTA) (800) 772-NSTA. Supplies books, posters, and CD-ROMs related to astronomy. Call to order a free catalog of NSTA books and materials.

The Planetary Society, 65 North Catalina Ave., Pasadena, CA 91106-9899 (818) 793-5100. Order the poster *An Explorer's Guide to Mars* with a map of Mars and many facts and photos.

Answer Key

Planet Data for Scale Model (page 6)

List Planets Largest to Smallest		Diameter Relative to Earth's	x 5 cm = Radius for Circle
1	Jupiter	11.2	56 cm
2	Saturn	9.4	47 cm
3	Uranus	4	20 cm
4	Neptune	3.9	19.5 cm
5	Earth	1.00	5 cm
6	Venus	.95	4.8 cm
7	Mars	.53	2.7 cm
8	Mercury	.38	1.9 cm
9	Pluto	.18	0.9 cm

Planets' Distances from the Sun (page 8)

Distance from sun	Mercury	Venus	Earth	Mars	Jupiter	Saturn	Uranus	Neptune	Pluto
Relative Earth's	0.4 AU	0.7 AU	1.0 AU	1.5 AU	5.2 AU	9.6 AU	19.3 AU	30.3 AU	39.7 AU

How Fast Are We Moving? (page 14)

Circumference (measured to nearest mm)	÷ Diameter	= Results
15.5 cm	5 cm	3.10
25.3 cm	8 cm	3.16
38 cm	12 cm	3.16

Diameter of Earth 7,973 miles X 3.14 = 25,035 miles (circumference) ÷ 24 hours = 1,043 mph. The dot on the Equator will be moving fastest on the globe as it is spun.

Answer Key (cont.)

Balloon Rocket (page 17)

The balloon remains at rest as long as the air is held inside it. When the air begins to rush out, it pushes the balloon forward (first law of motion). The more air in the balloon, the greater distance it will fly (second law). The balloon is pushed in the opposite direction of the air flow (third law).

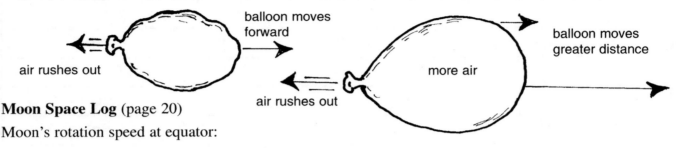

Moon Space Log (page 20)

Moon's rotation speed at equator:

<u>2160 miles</u> x 3.14 = <u>6782 miles</u> ÷ <u>656</u>   =   <u>10.34 miles per hour</u>
diameter   circumference hours in day   rotation speed at equator

Age on the moon would be the same as on Earth since it moves with the Earth around the sun.

Diameter of the Sun (page 30)

Diameter of sun—<u>870,000 miles</u> ÷ Earth's diameter—<u>7973 miles</u> = <u>109</u> x 10 cm = 1090 cm (10.9 m)

Rotation Speed of Planets (Answers for Space Logs of the Planets)

Categories	Mercury	Venus	Earth	Mars	Jupiter	Saturn	Uranus	Neptune	Pluto
Diameter in Miles: (kilometers)	3.050 (4,880)	7,563 (12,100)	7,973 (12,756)	4,246 (6,794)	89,365 (142,984)	75,335 (120,536)	31,938 (51,100)	30,938 (49,500)	1,438 (2,300)
Circumference in Miles: (kilometers)	9,577 (15,323)	23,748 (37,994)	25,035 (40,054)	13,332 (21,333)	280,606 (448,970)	236,552 (378,483)	100,285 (160,454)	97,145 (155,433)	4,515 (7,222)
Length of day in hours	1416 h	5832 h	24 h	25 h	10 h	11 h	17 h	16 h	153 h
Rotation Speed/ mph (kph)	7 (11)	4 (7)	1043 (1669)	533 (853)	28,061 (4,489)	21,505 (34,408)	5,899 (9,438)	6,072 (9715)	30 (47)

Mars Data (page 32)

Mars is closest to Earth at position 4/D and most distant at 12/L. Mars would look larger at the closest point (4/D) and smaller at 12/L. There are more positions in Mars' orbit since it takes longer than Earth (1.5 Earth years) to travel around the sun.

Jupiter's Moons (page 33)

Galileo saw four moons around Jupiter (his telescope was not good enough to see all 16 moons). His drawings showed the moons stayed close to Jupiter, sometimes appearing on one side and sometimes the other side of the planet, indicating they were rotating around it. When fewer than four moons could be seen, the missing moons were behind or in front of the planet and therefore invisible to Galileo.

Answer Key *(cont.)*

Comparing the Giant Planets (page 35)

The chart below shows a sample weight comparison of someone who is 87 pounds on Earth with the equivalent weight on Jupiter, Saturn, Uranus, and Neptune.

The rotation speed is so fast on these giant planets that they literally pull their atmosphere around as a beater does with cake batter. This creates tremendous wind forces in the atmosphere.

Data	Earth	Jupiter	Saturn	Uranus	Neptune
Surface Gravity	1.00 g	2.53 g	1.07 g	.91 g	1.16 g
Your Weight on . . .	87 lbs (39 kg)	220 lbs (99 kg)	93 lbs (42 kg)	79 lbs (36 kg)	101 lbs (45 kg)
Diameter Relative to Earth's	1.00	10.79	8.91	4.05	3.91
Rotation Speed at Equator	1,043 mph (1,669 kph)	28,061 mph (44,897 kph)	21.505 mph (34,408 kph)	5,899 mph (9,438 kph)	6,072 mph (9,715 kph)

The Planets Drawn to Scale (Earth = 5 mm)

The drawings of the planets below show the actual scale size to be used on the space logs.

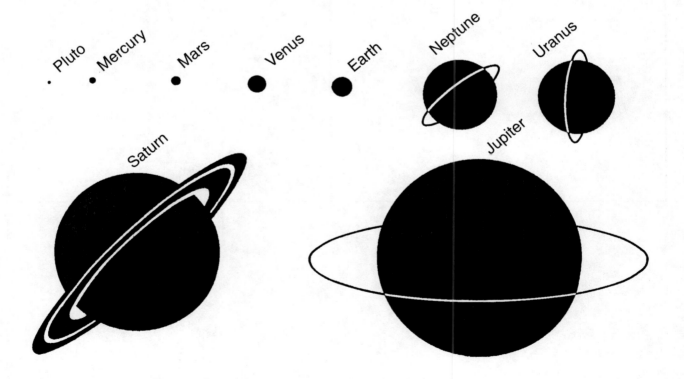

Answer Key *(cont.)*

Where is Planet X? (Page 37)

The arrows show the "star" which moved.

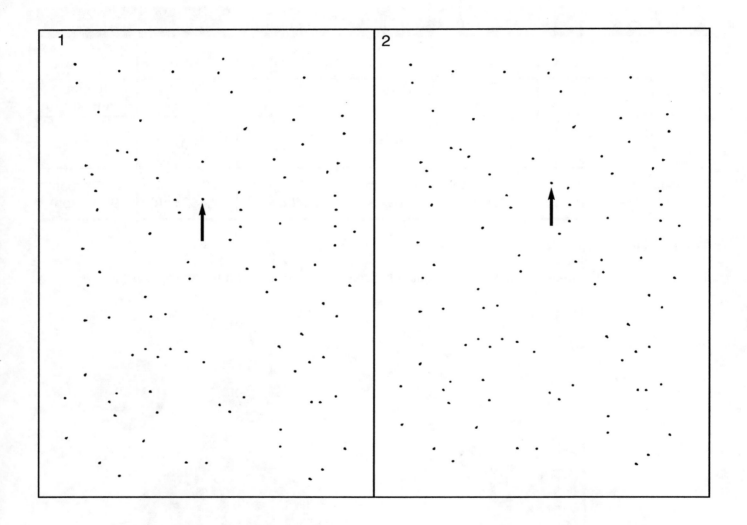